Peer Mediation

CONFLICT RESOLUTION IN SCHOOLS

REVISED EDITION

Student Manual

Fred Schrumpf

Donna K. Crawford

Richard J. Bodine

D1413571

RESEARCH PRESS
2612 North Mattis Avenue, Champaign, Illinois 61822
www.researchpress.com

The definition of peace on page 19 is quoted from "Gifts, Not Stars" (p. 553),
by George E. Lyon, in *Horn Book, September-October,* 1992.

Adaptations of the Red Riding Hood Story appearing on pages 40–42 are based on a retelling
in *Individual Development: Creativity,* by Leif Fearn, 1974, San Diego: Education Improvement Associates.
Currently published by Magic Circle Publishing, P.O. Box 1577, Spring Valley, CA 92077.

Cover design by Linda Brown
Typography by Tradewinds Imaging
Printed by McNaughton & Gunn

ISBN 0–87822–367–3
Library of Congress Catalog Number 96–69185

Contents

PEER MEDIATION FORMS   87

GLOSSARY   95

Basic Training

ACTIVITY 1

WELCOME AND OVERVIEW

Congratulations!

You are here because you have chosen to learn to be a peer mediator. Each of you has your own reasons for making that important choice.

Peer mediators possess qualities that contribute to their ability to help others:

▼ They have good judgment.

▼ They are respected by peers.

▼ They are someone other students can talk to and trust.

Each of you represents one or more of the various groups that make up our school. Our school has a variety of people, personalities, cultures, and ethnic groups. It is important that peer mediators represent this full spectrum of the student population, so during this training, please speak from your personal experience and for the peers you represent.

During this training, you will build upon your positive qualities and abilities. You will learn how to help others who are experiencing conflict to work together to resolve their problem.

This process of conflict resolution is called **mediation,**
and you will learn to be a **peer mediator**.

WHAT YOU WILL LEARN

During training, you will be actively involved in learning a great deal about the mediation process. Together we will investigate the following major topics:

▼ What mediation is

▼ Understanding conflict—nature of, origins of, and responses to conflict

▼ Principles of conflict resolution and peacemaking

▼ Communication skills

▼ The six-step mediation process

▼ Mediation practice

▼ How the peer mediation program will operate

At the end of training you will be a **peer mediator**.

GROUND RULES FOR TRAINING

You are here to learn to be peer mediators, and the expectation is that you will each be successful. Mediation is a powerful process, but it requires a high level of skill to use effectively. It also requires that each person learn to use the process in a way that fits his or her own personality. The training will be experiential, which means you will learn by doing. You will be trained to be true to a specific process, but you will also be asked to practice the process so you can make it work for you personally. Some of the adults here have used mediation, but there are no absolute "experts." We learn more about mediation each time we use the process, see others use it, or provide training.

During this training we are all here to learn and help others learn. You will be asked to try some things that may be new and strange to you. It is important that we all feel free to try these new things and that we help one another.

Let's all agree that we will not put anyone down or ridicule anyone's effort, but that we will encourage and help one another. We expect this to be hard work, but it will also be fun. We will all laugh because some of what happens will be funny, and we need to laugh. When you are finished with the training you will have skills few others have—you will be able to serve others as a **peacemaker**. So, during the training:

▼ Show respect for others.

▼ Be a good listener.

▼ Honor differences. Remember, we each represent
different groups as well as our own different experiences.

▼ Cooperate and help one another.

ACTIVITY 2

PEER MEDIATION: DEFINITION

WHAT IS MEDIATION?

Mediation is a communication process in which the people with the problem work together, with the assistance of a neutral third party, cooperating to resolve their conflict peaceably.

The **mediator** is the neutral third party. When students serve as mediators to assist other students, they are called **peer mediators**.

Mediation is an approach to resolve conflict in which the **disputants**—the people who disagree—have a chance to sit face-to-face and talk, uninterrupted, so each **point of view** is heard. After the problem is identified, the disputants create options for mutual gain and choose a **win-win** solution. They then finalize an **agreement** to behave in some way from that point forward.

PEER MEDIATION: BELIEFS

It takes cooperation and understanding to resolve conflicts. Peer mediation is based on the belief that in order to resolve conflicts constructively, those with the conflict must be willing to do as follows:

▼ Stay calm and control their anger, frustration, or other strong feelings.

▼ Focus on the problem and not blame the other person.

▼ Accurately state their feelings and wants.

▼ Respect and work to understand different points of view.

▼ Cooperate and create solutions that meet the needs of everyone involved.

The mediator helps the disputants behave in these constructive ways.

UNDERSTANDING CONFLICT

DEFINING CONFLICT WORKSHEET

PART 1

Conflict

Conflict

Conflict

Conflict

PART 2

Conflict

Conflict

CONFLICT HAPPENS WORKSHEET

Record two or three examples of conflicts you have experienced or know that others have experienced for each of the following settings.

HOME (with parents or other adults)

```

```

HOME (with brothers, sisters, other kids)

```

```

AT SCHOOL (with peers)

```

```

AT SCHOOL (with teachers, other adults)

```

```

AT SCHOOL (with rules, expectations)

```

```

IN THE NEWS

```

```

STATEMENTS ABOUT CONFLICT

Most of us have negative ideas about conflict, and these negative ideas often create barriers to our willingness or ability to deal with conflict. People live, work, and play together. To do so, people must understand the following ideas about conflict:

▼ Conflict is a part of everyday life.

▼ Conflict can be handled in positive or negative ways.

▼ Conflict can have either creative or destructive results.

▼ Conflict can be a positive force for personal growth and social change.

Therefore . . .

▼ Conflict will happen; violence does not have to happen.

▼ It is not our choice whether or not to have conflict.

▼ It is our choice how to act when we do have conflict.

RESPONSES TO CONFLICT WORKSHEET

Put a check mark (✓) in the boxes that show the responses that are most typical for you when you are in conflict with another person.

	Often	Sometimes	Never
Yell back or threaten the person	❏	❏	❏
Avoid or ignore the person	❏	❏	❏
Change the subject	❏	❏	❏
Try to understand the other side	❏	❏	❏
Complain to an adult	❏	❏	❏
Call the other person names	❏	❏	❏
Let the person have his or her way	❏	❏	❏
Try to reach a compromise	❏	❏	❏
Let an adult decide who is right	❏	❏	❏
Talk to find ways to agree	❏	❏	❏
Apologize	❏	❏	❏
Hit or push back	❏	❏	❏
Cry	❏	❏	❏
Make it into a joke	❏	❏	❏
Pretend my feelings are not hurt	❏	❏	❏

RESPONSES TO CONFLICT

Responses to conflict generally fall into one of three categories: soft responses, hard responses, or principled responses.

Soft Responses

Sometimes we respond to conflict in soft ways. Have you ever:

▼ Ignored a conflict, hoping it would go away?

▼ Denied that a conflict mattered to you?

▼ Withdrawn from a situation and not shared what you felt?

▼ Given in just to be nice?

Soft responses to conflict involve **avoidance**. People avoid conflict by withdrawing from the situation, ignoring the problem, or denying their feelings. Avoiding conflict may help in the short run—for instance, it might help someone keep from losing his or her temper. However, avoidance usually causes self-doubt and makes a person feel anxious about the future. In addition, because the conflict is never brought up, it can never be resolved.

Hard Responses

Sometimes we respond to conflict in hard ways. Have you ever:

▼ Threatened another person?

▼ Shoved or pushed someone out of frustration?

▼ Yelled words you really didn't mean?

▼ Hit someone or destroyed something out of anger?

Hard responses to conflict involve **confrontation**. Confrontation in response to conflict means a person expresses anger, verbal or physical threats, or aggression. It may also mean the person resorts to bribery or to punishments like withholding money, favors, or affection. These actions show a **win-lose** attitude toward conflict, or the attitude that one person must win and the other person must lose in a conflict. This attitude prevents cooperation and keeps people from reaching a mutually satisfying solution.

Principled Responses

A third type of response to conflict is a principled response. Have you ever:

▼ Listened with the intent to understand the other person's point of view?

▼ Cooperated with someone else without giving in?

▼ Shown respect for differences between you and another person?

▼ Looked for ways to resolve a problem that helped everyone involved?

A principled response to conflict involves **communication**. Communicating means participating in a common understanding, not necessarily agreeing. In order for people to cooperate, they must first communicate. People in conflict who seek first to understand the other person's side, then be understood, produce **win-win** solutions.

A principled response to conflict means both people get
their needs met, and no one loses.

ORIGINS OF CONFLICT

BASIC NEEDS

Understanding how to resolve a conflict begins with identifying the origin of the conflict. Most every dispute between people involves the attempt to meet certain **basic needs** for belonging, power, freedom, or fun.

▼ Our **BELONGING** need is met by developing and maintaining relationships with others where we have the opportunity to love, share, and cooperate.

▼ Our **POWER** need is met by achieving, accomplishing, and being recognized and respected.

▼ Our **FREEDOM** need is met by making choices in our lives.

▼ Our **FUN** need is met by laughing and playing.

We might think that people or situations cause us to act a certain way, but this belief is not true. We act the way we do because we are trying to meet our basic needs. Here are some examples:

Suppose you are upset because your friend is going to a party and you were not invited. You might get into a conflict with the friend because you are not getting your need for belonging met.

Suppose you are in conflict with a parent about the chores you must do around the house. This conflict might be the result of your need to have the freedom to make your own choices about how to spend your time.

You may be mad at the coach because you think you deserve more playing time, and her decision not to let you play is frustrating your power need—you think she doesn't recognize your ability and not playing deprives you of the chance to gain respect from your teammates and the fans.

BASIC NEEDS WORKSHEET

BELONGING

POWER

FREEDOM

FUN

❖

We are all born with the same four basic needs. However, the things we each choose in order to meet those needs may be different from what others choose. These different choices may cause a conflict, either because two people are trying to satisfy the same need in two different ways or because they are each trying to satisfy a different basic need.

LIMITED RESOURCES

When **resources** are limited, conflicts may result. Conflicts that involve limited resources are about time, money, property, or some combination of these things. For example, two classmates might be having a conflict over property when they are arguing about who will get to use a certain book they both want for a report.

Think of examples of conflicts you have experienced involving limited resources:

▼ A conflict about **money**

▼ A conflict about personal/school **property**

▼ A conflict about **time**

We each want money or property or time because we see these as things that allow us to satisfy our basic needs. If we have money, we can afford to do more (freedom, fun, belonging). We can buy things like great clothes, sports equipment, or audio-video products to gain recognition (power). When we have plenty of time, we can do our work (power) and also hang out with our friends (fun, belonging, freedom).

Resources are **wants** that we choose to satisfy our basic needs. The two students arguing over the book they both want for a report are likely each attempting to satisfy their power need: If they can write a quality report they will feel they have accomplished or achieved and they will likely be recognized by the teacher and perhaps others for doing so.

Unmet basic needs are at the heart of conflicts over limited resources.
If the parties can communicate, they can develop a plan to cooperate
and share the limited resource.

CULTURAL AND SOCIAL DIVERSITY WORKSHEET

Each of us has received a variety of gifts, making each of us unique. You probably like some gifts more than you like other gifts. You may even wish you could exchange some of your gifts: Some you can change, but many you cannot. Check the categories or fill in the blanks for those items that are most nearly true about you.

Gift of Race/Ethnicity
- ❏ African American
- ❏ Asian American
- ❏ European American
- ❏ Hispanic American
- ❏ Native American
- ❏ Other _____

Gift of Ability
- ❏ Artistic
- ❏ Leadership
- ❏ Mathematical
- ❏ Mechanical
- ❏ Musical
- ❏ Physical
- ❏ Verbal
- ❏ Other _____

Gift of Culture
Family practices in:
- ❏ Dress
- ❏ Food
- ❏ Holidays
- ❏ Language
- ❏ Other _____

Gift of Gender
- ❏ Female
- ❏ Male

Different Values

We all have different **values**. Values are the beliefs, convictions, priorities, and rules we follow. Differences in values may result in conflicts.

Conflicts involving values tend to be difficult to resolve because when people's values are different, they often perceive the dispute as a personal attack. When a person feels attacked, he or she often either withdraws or attacks—and neither of these reactions will likely de-escalate the conflict. For example, a student who values honesty in her friends will probably be very upset and angry if she learns that a friend has lied to her.

Our values are very much influenced by who we are and by our social environment. Our gender, our race, our social status, our ethnic group, our culture, and our abilities are differences that all play a part in forming our values. These differences are referred to as **cultural diversity** and **social diversity.** They also include diversity of religion, national origin, age, sexual orientation, and so on.

Values are wants that we use to guide our actions because we believe that they show us the best way to satisfy our needs. We may believe this because of our gifts or because we think our gifts are better than or not as good as another's gifts.

Unmet basic needs are at the heart of conflicts over different values.

The student who is angry because her friend lied to her is attempting to satisfy her belonging need, but she finds it difficult to share and cooperate with someone who is dishonest. Her friend may also be attempting to satisfy her belonging need, but she fears that if she is honest with her friend the truth will hurt her friend's feelings and the friend will become angry and choose to avoid her.

Resolving conflicts involving differing values does not mean the disputants have to change or align their values. They may need to agree to disagree, respectfully. Often a mutual acknowledgment that they see things differently is the first step toward a resolution.

When values are expressed as a behavior that limits another's basic rights, that behavior is inappropriate, and the rules of the school should prohibit it. A peer mediation may help the individuals in dispute plan a different, more acceptable behavior.

CONFLICT DIAGRAM

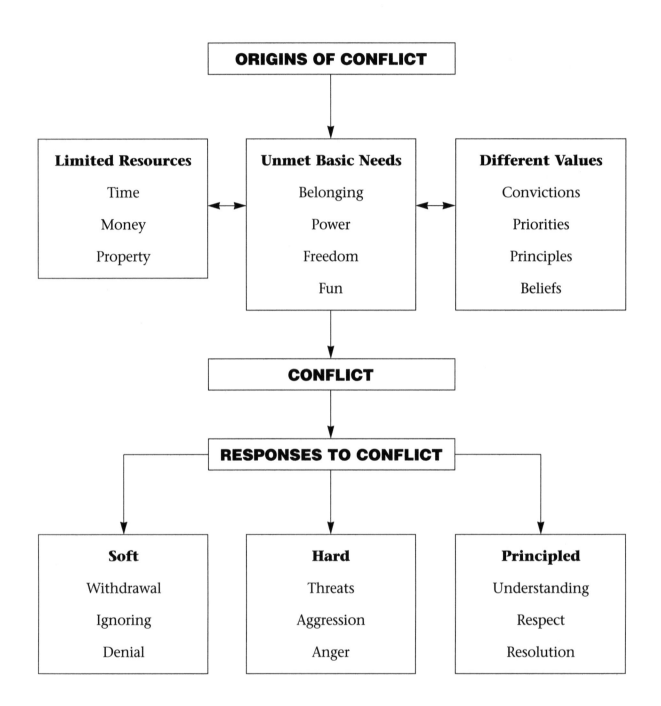

ORIGINS OF CONFLICT

Limited Resources

Time

Money

Property

Unmet Basic Needs

Belonging

Power

Freedom

Fun

Different Values

Convictions

Priorities

Principles

Beliefs

CONFLICT

RESPONSES TO CONFLICT

Soft

Withdrawal

Ignoring

Denial

Hard

Threats

Aggression

Anger

Principled

Understanding

Respect

Resolution

UNDERSTANDING PEACE AND PEACEMAKING

PEACE IS . . .

PEACE is that state when every person is able to survive and thrive without being hampered by conflict, prejudice, hatred, or injustice.

PEACE is that state when each individual fully exercises his or her responsibilities to ensure that all individuals fully enjoy all rights.

PEACE is a process of responding to diversity and conflict with tolerance, imagination, and flexibility; war is a product of our intent to stamp out diversity and conflict when we give up on the process of peace. George E. Lyon

 is balance and harmony.

Peacemaking is honoring yourself, honoring others, and honoring the environment. Peer mediators are peacemakers who also have the skills to help others make peace.

PEACE OR VIOLENCE WORKSHEET

1. What are some peacemaking behaviors students exhibit in your school?

2. What are some peacebreaking behaviors students exhibit in your school?

3. Is your world becoming more peaceful or more violent? Why?

4. What are some results of violence? On a person? On a school? On a community?

5. Why do you think your peers might choose to mediate a dispute?

6. Why do you think your peers might choose not to mediate a dispute?

When conflicts remain unresolved, violence may result.

The process of mediation is based on four principles of conflict resolution. **Peacemaking behaviors** are based on these principles because they allow disputants to reach agreements that honor themselves, the other person and, often, others around them, too. The agreement may also involve honoring the environment.

Principle 1: Separate the People from the Problem

This principle concerns behaviors in three areas:

> ▼ **Perceptions:** Each person in a conflict will view the conflict differently. For resolution it is important that each understand how the other views the problem.

> ▼ **Emotions:** People in conflict often have strong feelings about each other or about the problem. The expression of those feelings is important in gaining a full understanding of the problem. Because the expression of strong emotions by one person may provoke an equally strong expression from the other, it is important that while one person expresses emotions, the other listen and refrain from reacting.

> ▼ **Communication:** Conflict resolution requires that each of the individuals in the conflict talk about the conflict and listen to the other.

Principle 2: Focus on Interests, Not on Positions

This principle recognizes that individuals in conflict have different ideas about what should happen and that each has reasons to support his or her ideas.

> ▼ **Position:** What the disputant wants; may be expressed as a proposed solution or as a demand.

> ▼ **Interest:** A reason why the disputant wants what he or she wants or why the disputant thinks a particular solution will solve the problem.

Generally, each position is supported by several interests. When disputants focus discussion on positions, rarely are they able to reach a satisfactory agreement. But if they focus discussion on interests, they very often can find a resolution that satisfies both of their interests.

Principle 3: Invent Options for Mutual Gain

This principle recognizes that it is better for disputants to try to think of ideas that allow each person to gain than to argue over who will win and who will lose or simply to work on a compromise. The process used is **brainstorming**. Brainstorming is generating ideas without deciding.

Principle 4: Use Objective Criteria

This principle recognizes that applying standards allows disputants to accept an agreement. If each person thinks an idea is fair, he or she will likely commit to and keep the agreement.

Peer mediators help disputants behave according to these principles
of conflict resolution.

COMMUNICATION SKILLS

WHAT IS COMMUNICATION?

Communication occurs when a listener hears and understands a speaker's essential thoughts and feelings. Often, conflicts continue because of poor communication between people.

COMMUNICATION PITFALLS

A peer mediator facilitates communication between disputants. Following are some ways that the peer mediator can shut down, rather than facilitate, communication:

Interrupt

Offer advice

Judge

Ridicule

Criticize

Distract

Bring up your own experience

Be sure to avoid these common pitfalls.

In order to help disputants communicate, the peer mediator uses the following specific communication skills:

▼ Attending

▼ Summarizing

▼ Clarifying

Altogether, these skills are called **active listening**. This name signifies that listening requires one to be active and diligent, not passive.

Attending

Attending means using nonverbal behaviors to show you hear, that you are interested, and that you wish to understand. These nonverbal behaviors include such things as eye contact, facial expressions, gestures, and posture. Also included are very brief verbal utterances like "Hum!" "Uhm," "Uh-huh!" "OK!" "Wow!" and so forth. Generally, if you are leaning forward, smiling, nodding your head, and ignoring outside distractions, you are attending.

It is important for the peer mediator to attend to the disputant when he or she is speaking and to attend equally to each disputant during the mediation.

Summarizing

Summarizing means you do two things: You restate facts by repeating the most important points, organizing interests, and discarding extra information. Also, you reflect feelings about the conflict. It is very important when summarizing to recognize feelings in the situation as well as facts.

Clarifying

Clarifying means using open-ended questions or statements to get additional information and to make sure you understand. Some examples of open-ended questions include:

▼ How did you feel when that happened? *(question)*

▼ Do you have anything to add? *(question)*

▼ Tell me what happened next in the situation. *(statement)*

▼ What do you think is keeping you from reaching an agreement about this problem? *(question)*

Open-ended questions can be answered in many different ways and help keep people talking. The answer to a closed question provides little information and is often simply yes or no. Closed questions and statements such as the following tend to discourage people from further discussion:

▼ Did you feel angry when that happened?
(yes-or-no question)

▼ You've been fighting for a long time.
(no response needed)

▼ Do you think you can reach an agreement about this problem?
(yes-or-no question)

COMMUNICATION SKILLS DIAGRAM

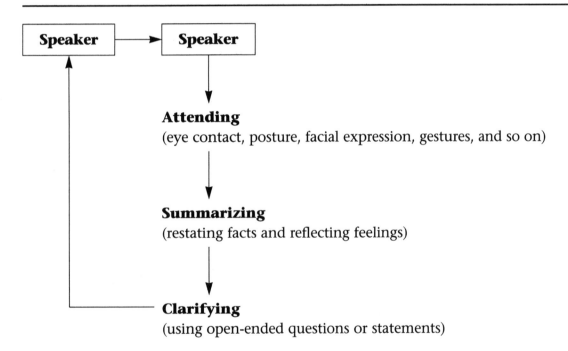

Speaker → **Speaker**

Attending
(eye contact, posture, facial expression, gestures, and so on)

Summarizing
(restating facts and reflecting feelings)

Clarifying
(using open-ended questions or statements)

Active listening is a continuous process that consists of attending, summarizing, and clarifying. A skilled active listener uses these three components to encourage a speaker to continue talking in order to give the listener a full opportunity to understand the message.

TALK ABOUT A CONFLICT WORKSHEET

Think about a conflict you have had recently and complete this worksheet.

1. What happened? Who is involved?

2. How do you feel about the situation?

3. How do you think the other person feels?

4. What do you want? What are some of your reasons?

5. What do you think the other person wants? Why?

6. How have you responded to the conflict? *(soft, hard, principled response)*

7. How has the other person responded? *(soft, hard, principled response)*

EFFECTIVE COMMUNICATION WORKSHEET

Use this checklist to evaluate your communication behaviors. Put a check mark (✓) in the box that shows the degree to which you use each of the behaviors listed.

	Often	Sometimes	Never
1. Do you make eye contact?	❏	❏	❏
2. Do you watch the person's body posture and facial expressions?	❏	❏	❏
3. Do you empathize and try to understand feelings, thoughts, and actions?	❏	❏	❏
4. Do you keep from interrupting and let the person finish, even when you think you already know what the person means?	❏	❏	❏
5. Do you ask questions to clarify information?	❏	❏	❏
6. Do you nod your head or use gestures to show interest?	❏	❏	❏
7. Do you listen, even if you do not like the person who is talking or agree with what the person is saying?	❏	❏	❏
8. Do you ignore outside distractions?	❏	❏	❏
9. Do you listen for and remember important points?	❏	❏	❏
10. Do you suspend judgment about what is said—do you remain neutral?	❏	❏	❏

QUALITIES AND ROLE
OF THE PEER MEDIATOR

STATEMENTS ABOUT ME WORKSHEET

Complete the statements by writing the first response that comes to mind.

1. My peers describe me as _____

2. I get frustrated with _____

3. One way I relax is _____

4. I feel disappointed when _____

5. My parents describe me as _____

6. I get angry when _____

7. A quality I expect in a friend is _____

8. I trust someone if _____

9. I feel discriminated against when _____

10. One way I show respect is _____

11. I control my anger by _____

12. I feel best when _____

13. I am good at _____

14. I am prejudiced toward _____

15. I will be an effective peer mediator because _____

The peer mediator is impartial.

A mediator is neutral and objective, a person who does not take sides.

The peer mediator is an empathic listener.

A mediator is skilled at listening with the intent of understanding what each disputant thinks and feels.

The peer mediator is respectful.

A mediator is able to treat both parties with respect and understanding, and without prejudice.

The peer mediator is trustworthy.

A mediator builds the confidence and trust of the disputants in the mediation process by keeping information private. A mediator does not discuss the problem with other peers. Also, a mediator allows the disputants to solve their own problem rather than imposing his or her own favored solution.

The peer mediator helps people work together.

A mediator is responsible for the mediation process, not the solution to the problem. The solution to the problem is the responsibility of the disputants. When the disputants cooperate, they are able to find their own solution.

OVERVIEW OF THE PEER MEDIATION PROCESS

STEPS IN PEER MEDIATION

STEP 1 Agree to Mediate

STEP 2 Gather Points of View

STEP 3 Focus on Interests

STEP 4 Create Win-Win Options

STEP 5 Evaluate Options

STEP 6 Create an Agreement

PREPARING FOR PEER MEDIATION

By preparing properly, you demonstrate a sense of control and establish a secure climate in which the disputants are able to communicate. You prepare for the session by arranging the physical environment and assembling materials.

Arranging the Physical Environment

Arrange the physical environment in the mediation room so that no one is at any kind of disadvantage. Doing so will help the disputants see you as not taking sides and will help them communicate better.

It is important to decide who will sit where before a mediation session begins and to arrange the chairs before the disputants arrive. In arranging the chairs, follow two guidelines:

▼ Position the disputants face-to-face across from each other.

▼ Position yourself at the head of the table between the disputants and nearest to the exit.

Assembling Materials

Before beginning a session, collect and have available the following items:

▼ **Peer Mediation Request**

One of the disputants (or another party, such as a teacher) completes this form before the mediation takes place. The form tells the mediator a little about the conflict and helps in scheduling the mediation.

▼ **Brainstorming Worksheet**

This is the form on which the mediator records all the disputants' ideas for solving the conflict. (You can use an easel pad instead of this worksheet.)

▼ **Peer Mediation Agreement**

When the disputants reach an agreement, the mediator fills out this form to show exactly what they have agreed to do. The disputants and mediator sign the agreement.

▼ **Pen or pencil**

▼ **Marker** (if using an easel pad)

***

The mediation forms you will need start on page 87 of this manual.

***

PEER MEDIATION PROCESS SUMMARY

STEP 1: AGREE TO MEDIATE
▼ Make introductions and define mediation.
▼ State the ground rules:
> Mediators remain neutral; they do not take sides.
> Mediation is private.
> Take turns talking and listening.
> Cooperate to solve the problem.
▼ Get a commitment from each disputant to mediate and follow the ground rules.

STEP 2: GATHER POINTS OF VIEW
▼ Ask each disputant (one at a time) to tell his or her point of view about the problem.
▼ Listen to each disputant and summarize following each disputant's statement.
▼ Allow each disputant a chance to clarify by asking:
> Do you have anything to add?
> How did you feel when that happened?
▼ Listen and summarize.

STEP 3: FOCUS ON INTERESTS
▼ Determine the interests of each disputant. Ask:
> What do you want? Why do you want that?
▼ Listen and summarize. To clarify, ask:
> What might happen if you don't reach an agreement?
> What would you think if you were in the other person's shoes?
> What do you *really* want?
▼ Summarize the interests. Say: "Your interests are _____ ."

STEP 4: CREATE WIN-WIN OPTIONS
▼ Explain brainstorming and state its rules:
> Say any idea that comes to mind.
> Do not judge or discuss ideas.
> Come up with as many ideas as possible.
> Try to think of unusual ideas.
▼ Write disputants' ideas on the Brainstorming Worksheet.

STEP 5: EVALUATE OPTIONS
▼ Ask disputants to nominate ideas or parts of ideas. Circle these on the Brainstorming Worksheet.
▼ Evaluate options by applying criteria:
> Is this option fair?
> Can you do it?
> Do you think it will work?

STEP 6: CREATE AN AGREEMENT
▼ Help disputants make a plan of action. Get specifics from each disputant: Who, what, when, where, how?
▼ Write the Peer Mediation Agreement. To complete the agreement, have each disputant summarize by asking: "What have you agreed to do?"
▼ Close the mediation.

The following case example illustrates how a peer mediator uses the six steps to help two students reach an agreement. In this situation, the mediation between Michael and Sondra has been requested by the school principal, Mr. Thomas.

Step 1: Agree to Mediate

Mediator: Hello, my name is _____, and I am the mediator assigned to conduct this session today. What are your names?

Sondra: My name is Sondra.

Michael: Michael.

Mediator: Michael and Sondra, I welcome you both to the mediation center. Mediation is a communication process in which the two of you will work together, with my assistance, cooperating to peaceably resolve your conflict. For mediation to work, there are ground rules to follow. First, I remain neutral—I will not take sides. Mediation is private—I will not talk about your problem with other students. Each of you will take turns talking, and when one talks, the other should listen. Last, you are expected to cooperate to solve the problem. Sondra, do you agree to mediate and follow the rules?

Sondra: Yes.

Mediator: Michael, do you agree to mediate and to follow the rules?

Michael: OK!

Step 2: Gather Points of View

Mediator: Sondra, tell me your point of view.

Sondra: Michael and I were arguing in the hallway. I got mad and threw my books at him. Then he shoved me against the lockers and was yelling at me when Mr. Thomas saw us. Mr. Thomas suspended Michael. I never fight with anyone—I just got so frustrated with Michael, I lost control.

Mediator: You were frustrated and threw your books at Michael. Mr. Thomas saw Michael shove you and suspended him. What did you think when that happened?

Sondra: I felt bad that Michael got in trouble because I started the fight. We aren't talking, and nothing I do seems to help.

Mediator: Sondra, you're sorry Michael was suspended, and you're still frustrated. Michael, tell me your point of view.

Michael: Sondra is always getting mad at me. She tells everyone on the tennis team I'm rude and selfish. I missed a practice, and she turns it into a war.

Sondra: You're irresponsible. You're either late for practice, or you don't even bother to come.

Mediator: Sondra, it's Michael's turn to talk. Please don't interrupt. Michael, you missed a tennis practice, and Sondra got angry. Tell me more about that.

Michael: Well, we're doubles partners. She takes the game much too seriously. She needs to lighten up. She thinks just because she's my tennis partner, I belong to her. She calls me a lot, but I don't want to be with only one girl all the time. I need my space.

Mediator: Michael, are you saying that you are concerned Sondra wants more from you than just being your tennis partner?

Michael: Yes. She doesn't want me to be with other girls.

Mediator: Sondra, do you have anything else you want to add?

Sondra: Michael takes me for granted. I want him to consider how I feel when he stands me up at practice.

Mediator: Sondra, you want Michael to understand your feelings when he doesn't come to practice and doesn't tell you he won't be there.

Sondra: Yes, that's what I want.

Mediator: Michael, do you have anything to add?

Michael: No.

Step 3: Focus on Interests

Mediator: Sondra, why do you think Michael doesn't tell you when he is not going to make practice?

Sondra: Well . . . he probably doesn't want to hear me yell and cry in front of his friends.

Mediator: Sondra, do you think yelling at Michael will help him get to practice?

Sondra: No, I guess not.

Mediator: Michael, what do you want?

Michael: I want her to stop getting so angry.

Mediator: You don't want Sondra to be mad at you. Michael, if Sondra stood you up for practice, how would you feel?

Michael: Oh, I would be worried she got hurt or something. I probably would be mad if I found out she did it on purpose.

Mediator: You'd be concerned that she was all right and upset if she did it on purpose. Michael, what do you really want?

Michael: What do you mean?

Mediator: Do you want to be Sondra's friend?

Michael: I want to be her friend, and I want to be her tennis partner. I don't want to be her boyfriend.

Mediator: You want to be Sondra's friend and tennis partner? Is standing her up for practice helping you get what you want?

Michael: No, it's not helping.

Mediator: Sondra, what do you want?

Sondra: I guess I've wanted Michael to be my boyfriend, and the more I try to make that happen the worse things get.

Mediator: Sondra, can you make Michael be your boyfriend?

Sondra: No, not if he doesn't want to be.

Mediator: Sondra, do you want to be Michael's tennis partner?

Sondra: Yes.

Mediator: Do you want to be his friend?

Sondra: I think so.

Step 4: Create Win-Win Options

Mediator: It sounds like you both want to be friends and tennis partners. Now I want you both to think about what you can do to help solve your problem. We'll make a list of possible solutions by brainstorming. The rules for brainstorming are to say any ideas that come to mind, even unusual ideas. Do not judge or discuss the ideas, and look for as many ideas as possible that might satisfy both of you. Ready? What can you do to solve this problem?

Michael: I could stop skipping practice . . .

Sondra: And let me know if you can't make it.

Michael: We could practice before school if we miss a practice.

Sondra: I could stop yelling at Michael.

Mediator: What else can you both do to solve the problem?

Michael: We could play tennis on Saturday mornings and then have lunch together.

Sondra: I could stop calling Michael just to talk.

Michael: I could take the tournament that's coming up more seriously . . . I really didn't think it mattered.

Mediator: Can you think of anything else?

Michael: No.

Sondra: No.

Step 5: Evaluate Options

Mediator: Which of these ideas will probably work best?

Michael: Well, practicing before school would work.

Sondra: If I don't yell at Michael and stop calling him all the time, he probably would like practice better.

Mediator: Can you do this?

Sondra: If I get upset about something, I could write Michael a note to explain . . . and then we could talk about the problem instead of arguing. Michael could do the same if he's upset about something.

Mediator: Michael, would this work for you?

Michael: It would be better than yelling.

Mediator: What else are you willing to do?

Michael: Well, we have this tournament coming up . . . I would be willing to practice before and after school and on Saturday mornings to make up for the times I've missed.

Mediator: Sondra, are you willing to do that?

Sondra: That practice schedule would be hard work, but I'll do it. I think we can win if we practice real hard. We also need to let each other know if we need to cancel.

Mediator: How would that work?

Michael: We could either call each other or leave notes in each other's lockers.

Mediator: Sondra, do you agree that would help?

Sondra: Yes.

Step 6: Create an Agreement

Mediator: You both seem to have agreed to practice before school, after school, and on Saturday. If either of you needs to cancel practice you will either call the other or leave a note. What time?

Sondra: How about at 7:30 in the morning and 4:00 after school and, say, 10:00 on Saturday?

Michael: OK.

Mediator: Where will you leave the notes for each other and when?

Michael: If we are canceling after-school practice we can put a note in the other person's locker at lunch. I guess we should call if we are canceling before school or on Saturday.

Sondra: That's good.

Mediator: Is there anything else you can agree to?

Sondra: I think that if we have a problem in the future we should write the other person a note explaining the problem and then talk about it.

Michael: I think that's fair.

Mediator: Is the problem solved?

Sondra: I think so.

Michael: Yeah.

Mediator: Michael, what have you agreed to do?

Michael: I've agreed to get serious about tennis and practice every day at 7:30 and at 4:00 and on Saturday morning, and to always show up unless I tell Sondra in advance. Also, I agree to talk with Sondra when there is a problem rather than just ignoring her.

Mediator: Sondra, what have you agreed to do?

Sondra: Practice before and after school every day and on Saturday, at 10:00, I think. I will stop calling Michael just to talk, and I will let him know when something is bothering me without yelling at him or trying to embarrass him.

Mediator: Please look over this agreement to be sure it is correct, and if it is, sign it.

(Sondra and Michael sign, and the mediator signs. The mediator shakes hands with Sondra, then Michael.)

Mediator: Thank you for participating in mediation. If you encounter other problems, please think about requesting mediation to help you. Would the two of you like to shake hands?

(Sondra and Michael shake hands.)

STEP 1: AGREE TO MEDIATE

STEP 1: AGREE TO MEDIATE

An effective opening to a mediation session sets the stage for the remainder of the session. You open the session by making introductions, defining mediation, stating the ground rules, and getting a commitment from each disputant to mediate and follow the ground rules.

1. Make introductions.

▼ Introduce yourself: "Hi! My name is _____ , and I will be your mediator."

▼ Ask each disputant for his or her name.

▼ Welcome disputants to mediation.

2. Define mediation.

▼ Use your own words to explain mediation to the disputants. For example: "Mediation is a communication process in which the people with the problem work cooperatively, with the assistance of a neutral third party, to resolve their conflict peaceably."

3. State the ground rules.

▼ Mediators remain neutral: "I will not take sides."

▼ Mediation is private: "I will not talk about you or your problem with other students. It is OK for you to tell others that you reached an agreement and what you agreed to, but don't talk about each other and the problem between you."

▼ Take turns talking and listening: "This means that while one of you is talking the other is expected to listen, and also that you will each have an equal opportunity to talk."

▼ Cooperate to solve the problem: "You will do your best to reach an agreement that considers both your interests."

4. Get a commitment from each disputant to mediate and follow the ground rules: "Do you agree to mediate and to follow the rules?"

STEP 2: GATHER POINTS OF VIEW

RED RIDING HOOD AND THE WOLF

Mediator: Hello, I am _____. I am your mediator. What is your name?

Red: I'm Red Riding Hood. They used to call me Little Red Riding Hood, but they don't anymore. You see, the Wolf and I have had this problem a long time, and I grew up.

Mediator: What is your name?

Wolf: I'm the Wolf.

Mediator: Welcome to the mediation center. I'm sorry it took you so long to find us. Mediation is a communication process where you, Red and Wolf, can work together, with my help as your mediator, to cooperate to solve the problem between you. The ground rules that make mediation work are as follows: I remain neutral—I do not take sides. Everything said in mediation is private. Each person takes turns talking without interruption. Finally, you will do your best to reach an agreement that considers both your needs. Red Riding Hood, do you agree to the ground rules?

Red: Yes.

Mediator: Wolf, do you agree to the ground rules?

Wolf: Yes, I do.

Mediator: Red Riding Hood, please tell what happened.

Red: Well, you see, I was taking a loaf of fresh bread and some cakes to my grannie's cottage on the other side of the woods. Grannie wasn't well, so I thought I would pick some flowers for her along the way. I was picking the flowers when the Wolf jumped out from behind a tree and started asking me a bunch of questions. He wanted to know what I was doing and where I was going, and he kept grinning this wicked grin and smacking his lips together. He was being so gross and rude. Then he ran away.

Mediator: You were taking some food to your grandmother on the other side of the woods and the Wolf appeared from behind the tree and frightened you.

Red: Yes, that's what happened.

Mediator: Wolf, please tell what happened.

Wolf: The forest is my home. I care about it and try to keep it clean. One day, when I was cleaning up some garbage people had left behind, I heard footsteps. I leaped behind a tree and saw a girl coming down the trail carrying a basket. I was suspicious because she was dressed in this strange red cape with her head covered up as if she didn't want anyone to know who she was. She started picking my flowers and stepping on my new little pine trees. Naturally, I stopped to ask her what she was doing and all that. She gave me this song and dance about going to her grannie's house with a basket of goodies.

Mediator: You were concerned when you saw this girl dressed in red picking your flowers. You stopped her and asked her what she was doing.

Wolf: That's right.

Mediator: Red Riding Hood, is there anything you want to add?

Red: Yes. When I got to my grannie's house the Wolf was disguised in my grannie's nightgown. He tried to eat me with those big ugly teeth. I'd be dead today if it hadn't been for a woodsman who came in and saved me. The Wolf scared my grannie—I found her hiding under the bed.

Mediator: You are saying the Wolf put on your grannie's nightgown so you would think he was your grannie and that he tried to hurt you?

Red: I said he tried to eat me.

Mediator: So you felt he was trying to eat you. Wolf, do you have anything to add?

Wolf: Of course I do. I know this girl's grannie. I thought we should teach Red Riding Hood a lesson for prancing on my pine trees in that get-up and for picking my flowers. I let her go on her way, but I ran ahead to her grannie's cottage. When I saw Grannie, I explained what happened, and she agreed her granddaughter needed to learn a lesson. Grannie hid under the bed, and I dressed up in Grannie's nightgown. When Red Riding Hood came into the bedroom, she saw me in the bed and said something nasty about my big ears. I've been told my ears are big before, so I tried to make the best of it by saying big ears help me hear her better. Then she made an insulting crack about my bulging eyes. This one was really hard to blow off because she sounded so nasty. Still, I make a policy to turn the other cheek, so I told her my big eyes help me to see her better. Her next insult about my big teeth really got to me. You see, I'm quite sensitive about them. I know when she made fun of my teeth I should have had better control, but I leaped from the bed and growled that my teeth would help me to eat her.

Mediator: So you and Grannie tried to play a trick on Red Riding Hood to teach her a lesson. Explain more about the eating part.

Wolf: Now, let's face it. Everyone knows no wolf could ever eat a girl, but crazy Red Riding Hood started screaming and running around the house. I tried to catch her to calm her down. All of a sudden the door came crashing open, and a big woodsman stood there with his axe. I knew I was in trouble . . . there was an open window behind me, so out I went. I've been hiding ever since. There are terrible rumors going around the forest about me. Red Riding Hood calls me the Big Bad Wolf. I'd like to say I've gotten over feeling bad, but the truth is I haven't lived happily ever after. I don't understand why Grannie never told my side of the story.

Mediator: You're upset about the rumors and have been afraid to show your face in the forest. You're also confused about why Grannie hasn't set things straight and has let the situation go on for this long.

Wolf: It just isn't fair. I'm miserable and lonely.

Mediator: Red Riding Hood, would you tell us more about Grannie?

Red: Well, Grannie has been sick—and she's been getting a little forgetful lately. When I asked her how she came to be under the bed she said she couldn't remember a thing that had happened.

Mediator: Grannie seems lately to have trouble remembering things, and she couldn't explain why she was under the bed.

STEP 2: GATHER POINTS OF VIEW

In this step, you will use the communication skills of active listening—attending, summarizing, and clarifying—to help you understand the disputants' situation and feelings and to help the disputants understand how each perceives the problem. Disputants may see the problem pretty much the same way or, more likely, they will have different points of view because they each perceive the problem differently and have different positions, or ideas, about how to solve the problem. In this step, you are not trying to get each disputant to agree on what happened but rather to share his or her own point of view and hear the point of view of the other.

1. Ask each disputant (one at a time) to tell his or her point of view about the problem:

 ▼ Please share your point of view.

 ▼ Please tell what happened.

2. Listen to each disputant and summarize following each disputant's statement.

3. Allow each disputant a chance to clarify by asking:

 ▼ Do you have anything to add?

 ▼ How did you feel when that happened?

4. Listen and summarize by asking for additional information if needed.

Additional questions to help gather points of view:

 ▼ How did you feel about the other person?

 ▼ What did you do?

 ▼ What were you thinking at the time?

 ▼ How long has the problem existed?

 ▼ What do you feel is the major problem?

 ▼ What are you doing now about the situation?

 ▼ How has your relationship changed?

 ▼ What did you want the other person to do that he or she didn't do?

 ▼ What did you want to do that you didn't do?

Since perceptions are reality, you need not be concerned with whether or not disputants are telling the "truth."

ACTIVITY 11

STEP 3: FOCUS ON INTERESTS

IDENTIFYING INTERESTS WORKSHEET

SITUATION	POSITION	INTERESTS
1. Marcus shouts at Tyrone, "You can't apply for the same job I did. There's only one opening, and I was there first!" Tyrone yells, "I deserve that job, too!"		
2. Lisa yells at her sister, Kara, "You can't ride my bike to school anymore. It's never here when I want it!" Kara yells, "I'm riding your bike—you almost never use it!"		
3. Diana is mad at her boyfriend, Jerome, and says, "If you go out with Rachel, I'll never speak to you again." Jerome yells back, "Rachel is a friend. I'm not her boyfriend!"		
4. Juan is upset with Malcolm: "If you keep asking me for answers in math class, I'll report you to the teacher." Malcolm shouts, "Go ahead—I'll report you when you ask me answers in science!"		
5. Keisha says to Natalie, "You can't go on the canoe trip because you can't swim like the rest of us." Natalie cries, "I don't need to swim like you. I'm going anyway!"		

44

STEP 3: FOCUS ON INTERESTS

In this step, your goal is to search for interests that join both disputants. Common or compatible interests serve as the building blocks for an agreement. Unless interests are identified, disputants probably will not be able to make an agreement they can both keep. Do not move on to Step 4 until you find out what the interests are.

1. Determine the interests of each disputant. Ask:

▼ What do you want? Why do you want that?

2. Listen and summarize. To clarify, ask:

▼ What might happen if you do not reach an agreement?

▼ What would you think if you were in the other person's shoes?

▼ What do you *really* want?

▼ Is *(Example: fighting)* getting you what you want?

▼ Why has the other disputant not done what you expect?

3. Summarize the interests. Say:

▼ Both of you seem to agree that _____ .

▼ Your interests are _____ .

STEP 4: CREATE WIN-WIN OPTIONS

STEP 4: CREATE WIN-WIN OPTIONS

Many possible ideas exist for resolving a conflict. However, when we are upset or frustrated, we often do not consider all of our options. In this step, you will help disputants create, through brainstorming, a number of options that could potentially solve their problem.

1. **Explain that brainstorming will help disputants find solutions that satisfy both parties.**

2. **State the rules for brainstorming:**

   ▼ Say any ideas that come to mind.

   ▼ Do not judge or discuss the ideas.

   ▼ Come up with as many ideas as possible.

   ▼ Try to think of unusual ideas.

3. **Tell disputants to try to think of ideas that will help both of them. Write their ideas on a Brainstorming Worksheet.**

Additional questions to help the brainstorming process along:

   ▼ What other possibilities can you think of?

   ▼ In the future, what could you do differently?

   ▼ What could be done to resolve this dispute?

STEP 5: EVALUATE OPTIONS

STEP 5: EVALUATE OPTIONS

Your main task in this step is to help disputants evaluate and improve on the ideas they created during brainstorming in Step 4. It is also important that the disputants apply objective criteria when deciding whether to keep or reject an option. This helps to ensure that they will be able to reach an agreement that both are likely to honor.

1. **Ask disputants to nominate ideas or parts of ideas they are willing to do in order to help solve the problem. Circle their responses on the Brainstorming Worksheet.**

2. **Evaluate the circled options and invent ways to improve the ideas by using one or more questions (criteria). Ask:**

   ▼ Is this option fair?

   ▼ Can you do it?

   ▼ Do you think it will work?

   ▼ Does the option address the interests of each of you? Of others?

   ▼ What are the consequences of deciding to do this?

   ▼ What if one person did _____? Could you do _____?

   ▼ What are you willing to try?

STEP 6: CREATE AN AGREEMENT

STEP 6: CREATE AN AGREEMENT

In this step, the peer mediator helps disputants create a sound agreement. A sound agreement is:

▼ Effective: It fairly resolves the major issues for each disputant.

▼ Mutually satisfying: Both disputants think it is fair.

▼ Specific: Answers who, what, when, where, and how.

▼ Realistic: The plan is reasonable and can be accomplished by the disputants.

▼ Balanced: Each person agrees to be responsible for something.

1. **Help disputants make a plan of action. Get specifics from each disputant: Who, what when, where, how. Ask:**

▼ What are you willing to do to solve this problem?

▼ Is the problem solved?

▼ What have you agreed to do?

2. **Write the Peer Mediation Agreement. To complete the agreement, have each disputant summarize by asking: "What have you agreed to do?"**

3. **Close the mediation:**

▼ Review the agreement form with both parties and make any changes.

▼ Sign the form and ask each party to sign.

▼ Thank disputants for participating in mediation, congratulate each for working to reach an agreement, and invite them to use mediation in the future.

▼ Shake hands with each disputant and invite disputants to shake hands with each other.

SAMPLE PEER MEDIATION AGREEMENT

Date ___11/13/96___

We voluntarily participated in a mediation. We have reached an agreement that we believe is fair and that solves the problem between us. In the future if we have problems that we cannot resolve on our own, we agree to come back to mediation.

Name ___Heather___   Name ___Andrew___

Agrees to act calmer and not yell at Andrew if a problem happens in the future.

Agrees to talk with Andrew first to check things out and will try not to jump to conclusions.

Agrees to talk with the principal today to see if he can get Heather's Gameboy.

If the principal refuses to return the Gameboy, Andrew agrees to ask the principal to accept Andrew's Gameboy in place of Heather's.

Agrees to return Heather's Gameboy to her or give her his Gameboy until such time as the principal agrees to release Heather's.

Signature ___Heather___   Signature ___Andrew___

Mediator signature ___Rodney Anderson___

Mediator signature ___Rachel Sharp___

ACTIVITY 15

CO-MEDIATION PRACTICE

WHAT IS CO-MEDIATION?

In **co-mediation,** two mediators work as a team to facilitate the mediation process. Co-mediators act as a single mediator, managing the process while supporting each other. In the co-mediation model, the team members perform two responsibilities:

▼ One member of the team actively facilitates the six-step mediation process.

▼ The other member of the team observes the process and supports the teammate.

Supporting a teammate involves monitoring the process to help make sure that the mediator is remaining neutral, that he or she is summarizing the statements of the disputants, that the ground rules are being followed, and so on. It also involves paying close attention to what is happening and being prepared at all times to help your teammate if he or she seems to be stuck. Often someone who is only observing can more easily think of a question that might help move the mediation toward a resolution because that person is not thinking about what has to be done in the particular step of the process.

Co-mediation works best when the two team members equally share these two responsibilities. One member of the team facilitates Steps 1, 3, and 5 while the other member observes and supports. For Steps 2, 4, and 6, the facilitation and support responsibilities are exchanged.

In co-mediation, the two mediators must decide in advance how they will work together. Co-mediators should decide the following questions:

▼ Who will facilitate Steps 1, 3, and 5, and who will facilitate Steps 2, 4, and 6?

▼ How will the observer help the facilitator? (How will he or she tell the facilitator he or she forgot to do something important, how will he or she offer suggestions, and so forth.)

Remember, as co-mediators your job is to help each other.
The two of you will model cooperation for the disputants.

SUPPORT FOR PEER MEDIATION AND PEER MEDIATORS

Things to Remember

Being a peer mediator is not always easy. Mediation is always a challenge. It is important to be positive and optimistic, even though a mediation is difficult or the outcome is not as you expect. Remember, you are there only to offer your skilled assistance.

> The problem belongs to the disputants—they own it and are the only ones who can solve it.

The times when mediation seems difficult or frustrating can become times of growth and change for everyone. Take the opportunity to talk with other peer mediators or adult staff members and share your thoughts and feelings. Remember that you promised to keep the information of the mediation private and that you must respect that promise when you have these discussions.

> If there is honest communication, thinking will be expanded and boundaries will be broken.

Encouraging another's efforts, sharing perspectives, and cooperating to solve human problems is a lifelong challenge. Through mutual support and respect, everyone will become stronger and better able to reach common goals. As Gandhi said, "If we are to reach real peace in this world, we shall have to begin teaching cooperation to the children."

> You have the knowledge and skills to teach peace to others through your assistance and your example.

Advanced Training

ACTIVITY 17

SOCIAL AND CULTURAL DIVERSITY

UNDERSTANDING INDIVIDUAL DIFFERENCES

To be an effective mediator you need to know yourself and your own biases. We all have certain preferences about food, music, clothes, sports, movies, and so on. There are also people and personalities we like more than others. These are examples of differences that we choose. There are also differences that we do not choose. Your gender, skin color, social status, religion, abilities, and national origin make you different from everyone else.

As a mediator, it is important to reflect on and understand individual differences. How do you view and interact with individuals who are different from you?

Think of all the different types of students who go to your school. Think of their different backgrounds, values, and interests. The diversity of your school will occur in any or all of the following categories:

▼ Diversity of culture
       Skin color
       Religion
       National origin

▼ Diversity of social status

▼ Diversity of gender

▼ Diversity of ability
       Physical
       Mental

How do you represent the diversity of the school?

How does it feel to be a member of your group?

PREJUDICE, BIAS, AND DISCRIMINATION

Usually, personal differences contribute to personal conflicts. If we are judged or judge others based on age, race, gender, abilities, social class, religion, or sexual orientation, that is **prejudice** or **bias**. When we act on our prejudice it becomes **discrimination**, which is harmful to others and keeps people from meeting their basic needs.

- ▼ Can you think of a time when you felt you were discriminated against?

- ▼ Can you think of a time when you discriminated against another person?

- ▼ As a mediator, in what conflict situations might it be hard for you to remain neutral?

- ▼ As a mediator, what type of person or what attitude held by a person might make it hard for you to remain neutral?

In your role as a peer mediator you help disputants understand individual differences—this understanding is essential to finding common interests. Further, through your sensitivity, you can become a powerful model to help others learn to respect individual differences. This respect promotes cooperation and in turn makes resolution possible.

BIAS AWARENESS

BIAS SELF-EVALUATION WORKSHEET

Here are some statements to reflect on about biased and nonbiased behaviors.
Rate each of the following items as follows:

1 = I have not thought about this.
2 = I do not do this.
3 = I do this to some extent.
4 = I do this consistently.

1 2 3 4   I do not put down or joke about people because of their culture, skin color, religion, country of origin, gender, or social class.

1 2 3 4   I do not put down or joke about people because of their abilities, disabilities, or physical appearance.

1 2 3 4   I avoid making generalizations about people that become stereotypes for all, such as "Fat people are lazy" or "Females are irrational."

1 2 3 4   I question books, movies, and the media when they present sexist and racist statements or assumptions.

1 2 3 4   I bring it to the attention of my peers if I hear negative comments or jokes about people based on individual differences (skin color, ability, sexual orientation, and so on).

1 2 3 4   I bring it to the attention of adults or peers if I see sexual harassment or gender discrimination.

CULTURAL DIVERSITY AND CLIQUES

A CLIQUE IS . . .

▼ A circle or set of friends

▼ To associate together

▼ To act with others of common interests

There are many **cliques** in every school. Groups of students join together in friendships due to similar interests. Some of these groups are easily identified.

If you are in a certain clique, you feel like an "insider." If you are not in a certain clique, you may feel like an "outsider." Often people feel like outsiders because they are different from the dominant group or they do not have access to that group.

Many conflicts arise because of insider/outsider status. Often insider groups make outsiders feel they do not belong. Groups or cliques are often based on preferences and common interests, and exclusion is natural. But exclusion may also be based on discrimination. If so, the group or clique is not defensible in a school.

Mediators often deal with conflicts between insiders and outsiders. Mediators can facilitate an exchange of feelings and help disputants differentiate between issues of preference and issues of discrimination.

STEREOTYPES

STEREOTYPING IS . . .

▼ A fixed notion or idea about a person or group—
an oversimplified generalization about a person
or group

▼ The basis for prejudice

▼ Limiting

▼ Not true for all individuals

Stereotypes usually play out in the form of discrimination. Ask yourself:

▼ Why has a woman never been President of the
United States? An African-American?

▼ Do you think Franklin D. Roosevelt would have
been elected president if he had been in a wheelchair
during his first campaign?

Stereotypes are a factor in many conflicts.

RESOLVING CROSS-CULTURAL CONFLICTS

CULTURAL TRAITS WORKSHEET

For each item, circle the number on the continuum that indicates where you fit with regard to each cultural trait.

Rational (stick to the facts)	1 2 3 4 5	**Emotional** (feelings are most important)
Competitive	1 2 3 4 5	**Cooperative**
Willing to admit error	1 2 3 4 5	**Interested in saving face**
Open to change	1 2 3 4 5	**Reluctant to change**
On task/on time (want specific details)	1 2 3 4 5	**Flexible** (general commitment OK)
Forgive easily	1 2 3 4 5	**Want payback/restitution**
Prefer direct communications	1 2 3 4 5	**Prefer nonverbal/indirect communications**

These are just some of the differences in how people view conflict or act in conflict situations. Different extremes of different traits might be more associated with one gender or with certain cultural groups, but remember what you have learned about stereotypes—there are always exceptions to such generalizations. As a mediation session proceeds, you will usually be able to determine what is important to each disputant.

QUESTIONS FOR RESOLVING CONFLICT

The following questions may help resolve conflict between disputants with obvious cultural diversity. The step or steps in the process where the question is likely to be appropriate are suggested.

1. What needs to happen to resolve the conflict?

   (Ask during Step 2 and/or Step 5.)

2. What have you gained or lost as a result of the conflict?

   (Ask during Step 2 and/or Step 3.)

3. What are your reasons for taking the position you did?

   (Ask during Step 3.)

4. What needs to happen to reestablish communication and trust?

   (Ask during Step 3, Step 4, Step 5, and/or Step 6.)

5. What would be a fair solution for you?

   (Ask during Step 5.)

6. What different attitudes or new actions would help improve the relationship between the two of you?

   (Ask during Step 4, Step 5, and/or Step 6.)

CONFRONTING PREJUDICE

ABOUT PREJUDICE

As a trained peer mediator, you have become aware of the **social** and **cultural diversity** that exists in your school. You are aware that differences can be either celebrated or used to separate and isolate people.

Every day, you probably hear remarks and see actions that discriminate and devalue certain people or groups of people in your school. Often you may feel uncomfortable or "on the spot" when you hear a harassing statement.

▼ When and how do you confront these statements?

▼ How do you communicate with a peer without causing him or her to feel attacked or put down?

▼ How do you communicate across differing beliefs without escalating a conflict?

Following are examples of typical statements that might be heard in a school:

1. As a group of girls are walking down the hall past your locker, you hear this comment from two guys standing nearby: "Look at Mary—she is definitely a 10, but her friend Andrea is more like a 4."

2. After school, while waiting at the bus stop you hear someone say: "That other bus has all those low-life trailer park kids."

3. In history class, during a discussion about the presidency someone says: "A woman should never be President of the United States. Women are too emotional and irrational to be President."

4. In the cafeteria you hear someone at your table say: "Black students in this school aren't very smart. Hardly any of them make the honor role."

❖

How might you respond in these situations?

STEPS FOR CONFRONTING PREJUDICE

1. Stay calm.

2. Summarize what you heard.

   ▼ "Did I hear you say _____?"

3. Seek clarification.

   ▼ "Can you tell me more about what you meant by _____?"

4. Share your point of view and why you believe this.

   ▼ "Well, the way I think about it is _____."

   ▼ "When you made that comment, I felt _____."

5. Ask the reasons for the person's point of view.

   ▼ "On what do you base your opinion?"

   ▼ "Is what you believe true for everyone?"

6. Try to find common ground.

   ▼ "It seems we both think that _____."

7. Thank the other person for listening.

CAUCUSING

WHAT IS CAUCUSING?

Caucusing is a tool that mediators may use in certain situations in order to help disputants work toward an agreement. Caucusing may be viewed as a "time-out" in the mediation process. In the mediation process, the disputants work face-to-face to reach an agreement. In a caucus, the mediators meet individually with each disputant.

A caucus may take place anytime during the mediation process and, although this is not usually the case, may occur more than once. Normally, caucusing will not be used at all, but it can be very effective if needed. It is the mediators' responsibility to decide whether or not a caucus is necessary.

REASONS FOR CAUCUSING

Caucusing can be used in a number of ways:

▼ To uncover information or clarify details that disputants may be willing to reveal only in private

▼ To move beyond an impasse

▼ To deal with issues of diversity or reduce tensions between disputants

▼ To explore options or the consequences of choosing particular options

▼ To help disputants understand the best outcome they can hope for if they choose not to work together to achieve a mutually satisfactory agreement

▼ To allow disputants time to think alone and reflect

▼ To build trust in the peer mediators and/or the mediation process

GUIDELINES FOR CAUCUSING

1. Meet individually with each disputant. (Co-mediators stay together as a team.)

   ▼ "We want to meet with each of you alone."

2. During the individual meetings, use the procedures in Step 2 (Gather Points of View), Step 3 (Focus on Interests), and Step 4 (Create Win-Win Options), depending on the situation.

3. Before returning to the joint session, be sure you have a clear understanding of what information the disputants do not want revealed. All statements made during caucusing are private unless the disputant agrees that the information can be shared.

   ▼ "Everything said when we are alone is private.
     I will not share anything said with the other disputant
     unless you give me permission."

4. When the mediation session resumes, summarize what happened in the mediation prior to the caucus, reveal or cause to be revealed any information the disputants want revealed from the caucus, and resume the mediation at the point you called for the caucus.

UNCOVERING HIDDEN INTERESTS

ABOUT HIDDEN INTERESTS

You might think determining what is at the bottom of a conflict is an easy matter, but often what the conflict appears to be about is not the only issue involved. People sometimes have **hidden interests** in a conflict situation—and often these hidden interests are unmet basic psychological needs for belonging, power, freedom, or fun.

During the basic training, you learned that conflicts frequently appear to be about limited resources or different values, perhaps involving diversity issues. However, the conflict is often really about unmet basic needs. For example:

> Suppose Robert is upset because his friend LaToya has not repaid some money she borrowed. Here it appears that the conflict between Robert and LaToya is caused by limited resources (in other words, a lack of money). But when LaToya offers to pay the money back in installments over a few weeks, Robert refuses to accept her solution. In actuality, Robert may view LaToya's failure to repay the loan as demonstrating a lack of respect for him and a lack of appreciation for their friendship. His needs for power and belonging are threatened. The conflict is unlikely to be resolved until Robert's unmet needs are recognized.

> Suppose Angela places a high value on honesty in friendships. She is angry with her friend Maria because Maria lied to her. In mediation, Angela will not accept Maria's explanations. She may make statements about Maria's ethnicity. Is this conflict the result of different values about honesty? Maybe yes and maybe no. Angela may be bothered less by the clash of values than by the idea that she feels she must cut herself off from Maria because Maria lied. In other words, Angela's need for belonging may be threatened. Any resolution to this problem will likely involve helping Angela decide if she wants to accept Maria as a friend.

Suppose Greg and Dimitri, who have been the best of friends, suddenly appear to be adversaries. Dimitri seems not to want to associate with Greg, an idea Greg has difficulty understanding. Actually, Dimitri likes Greg but feels that Greg does not consider his ideas or wishes. When they are together, having fun, Dimitri believes they always do what Greg wants to do. Dimitri increasingly has come to see this as both a lack of respect for him and as Greg's controlling their relationship. A resolution that would reunite these friends would need to consider Dimitri's concerns about freedom and respect.

Think about an iceberg in the ocean. We know that what is visible of the iceberg is only part, actually a small part, of the whole iceberg. The tip or visible part of the iceberg is like that part of a conflict that is not hidden—what the dispute seems to be about or what the disputants tell us the problem concerns. In the conflict, we see the positions people take and the demands that they make. Underneath the surface of the ocean is the major part of the iceberg. If ships are not aware of what lies under the tip of the iceberg, the ship will crash. (Remember the Titanic!) Just as with an iceberg, in a conflict the mediator often must probe below the surface of the conflict to explore what is underneath.

Hidden interests are often layered. The first layer may be fears or beliefs founded in prejudice or stereotypes. This layer often offers little to bring the disputants together because the fears and beliefs are rarely shared. Under this layer are the real interests, which are based on the psychological needs for belonging, power, freedom, and fun.

To resolve a conflict, a peer mediator helps disputants look under the surface for the real reasons for the problem. An important part of your job as mediator is to help disputants determine what is really causing the conflict. If you do not, the agreements you help disputants reach are unlikely to be lasting because they do not solve the REAL problem.

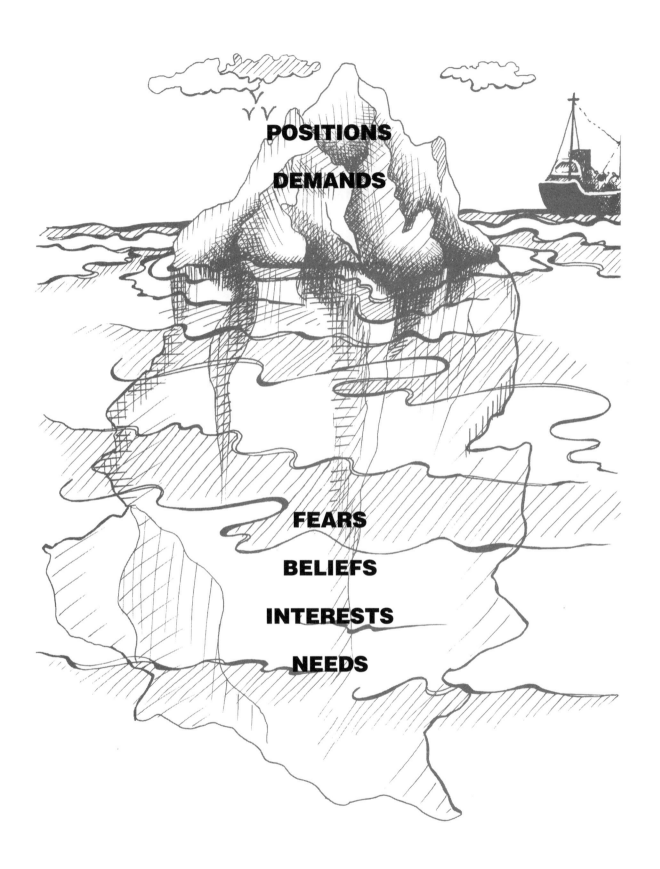

POSITIONS

DEMANDS

FEARS

BELIEFS

INTERESTS

NEEDS

69

HIDDEN INTERESTS DIAGRAM

Belonging

Fun

UNMET BASIC NEEDS

Power

Freedom

70

UNDERSTANDING ANGER

ABOUT ANGER

Everyone gets angry, upset, frustrated, or irritated by something. Have you ever heard someone remark that "She really knows how to push my buttons" or "He makes me so hot (angry)"? This means that the other person seems to know exactly what to do or say to trigger the speaker's anger. We might think of the words, actions, or both that provoke our anger as our personal **hot buttons**.

Often the people closest to us, our family and/or friends, can really push our hot buttons and really bug us. Sometimes it is people in charge or what they do with that authority that makes us angry.

The first step in learning to help others manage their anger
is to learn about our own anger.

ANGER WORKSHEET

Answer the following questions to help you understand your own personal anger.

1. Who are the people who really bug you, who push your hot buttons? Make a list of names, and after each name indicate what the person does or does not do that irritates you.

2. Describe the circumstances for the last three times you remember being angry.

3. Describe how you responded in each of those circumstances. Did your response escalate or deescalate the situation?

COOL BUTTONS: CONTROLLING YOUR ANGER WORKSHEET

1. Breathe deeply.

2. Count to 10.

3. Keep on counting and breathing deeply.

4. Visualize a calm and relaxing place.

5. Use positive self-talk and affirm yourself.

6. _____

7. _____

8. _____

9. _____

10. _____

❖

Why is it important to cool off before you mediate or negotiate a conflict?

PROCESSING ANGER

Anger is a strong human emotion signaling that one or more of our basic needs (belonging, power, freedom, fun) are not being met. Although most people think of anger as being a negative feeling, it is really neither good nor bad. The way people choose to process their anger can have either positive or negative outcomes, however.

Nonassertion

One way to process anger is by turning it inward, or **nonassertion**. People who behave this way are often depressed. In addition, because they never express their anger, no one ever knows what they think or want. As a result, they rarely get their needs met.

Aggression

Another way to process anger is **aggression**. Being aggressive means verbally or physically attacking another individual. This includes fighting, yelling, name-calling, put-downs, and so forth. Generally, aggression turns people off, or they choose to react in a similarly aggressive way, and the problem just gets worse.

Passive Aggression

A third way to process anger is **passive aggression**. People behaving this way look calm on the outside but are really angry inside. They might show anger by rolling their eyes, interrupting, or refusing to cooperate. Others tend to avoid passive aggressive people or choose to get angry in return.

Assertion

Still another way to process anger is **assertion**. Assertive people know they are angry and choose to express that feeling in an appropriate way. They know what they want and need, and can ask for it without showing disrespect for other people's wants and needs. Dealing with anger by being assertive makes it much more likely that people will be able to cooperate and reach a mutually satisfying solution.

As a peer mediator, you can help people process their anger through assertion— not nonassertion, aggression, or passive aggression.

HOW DO YOU DEAL WITH ANGRY PEOPLE?

▼ Listen to them.

▼ Affirm their feelings.

▼ Clarify their interests and needs.

▼ Don't take their anger personally.

SUGGESTIONS FOR DEALING WITH ANGER IN MEDIATION

1. Remind disputants of the ground rules.

   ▼ "You both agreed to take turns talking and listening."

2. Remind disputants that they agreed to cooperate to solve the problem.

   ▼ "You agreed to cooperate to solve the problem.
   Is what you are saying or doing helping you to cooperate?"

3. Use your active listening skills: Attend to the speaker, summarize what you hear to let the disputant know that he or she has been heard, and affirm or reflect the feelings expressed.

   ▼ "When _____ happened, you were very upset with _____."

4. Ask disputants to relax and take a few deep breaths.

5. Take a break to allow disputants to cool off and return to the mediation at a later time, perhaps even the next day.

6. Clarify interests and focus the mediation session on finding a plan to satisfy those interests rather than focusing on what happened.

7. Caucus with each disputant. Try to find out what the individual disputants want and if they think the anger is helping them get what they want. Coach them how to express their interests to each other.

ADVANCED COMMUNICATION SKILLS

REFRAMING

Reframing means listening to one disputant's hostile, angry, negative, accusing, or demanding statement and translating that statement into a productive statement of concern to which you as the mediator and the other disputant can respond. Often reframing means focusing the statement on the problem, not on the persons involved. The mediator offers the disputants a different way of viewing the situation. Reframing helps to tone down an emotional response (often name-calling or put-downs) and make communication more constructive. Reframing is based on the idea that every strong statement contains some underlying interest or concern that prompted the strong statement. Also, the speaker usually wants to be heard and expects a constructive response to his or her statement.

How to Reframe

1. Listen to the statement.

2. Remove the "garbage" (the inflammatory language).

3. Recognize the emotions involved and state who owns these emotions.

4. Try to understand the speaker's interest(s) or concern(s).

5. Restate the message as a concern about the problem, especially about meeting basic needs.

For example:

Disputant: She's got a big mouth, and she's a dirty liar.

Mediator: You seem upset, and you have a concern about people knowing the truth.

Disputant: Right, she has been telling everyone that I'm cheap and tight with my money, when in fact for the past 2 months she has owed me $20.00.

Mediator: It sounds like you're frustrated and would like a fair settlement of the money issue as soon as possible.

Practice Statements

1. I'm sick of her always telling me what to do. She acts like my mother all the time.

2. He and his friends are jerks. They always put me and my friends down. They think they own the school. They better stop, or else I'm gonna mess up their stuff.

3. Every time he sees me in the hall he just stares at me like he wants to get into it with me. He is not as great as he thinks he is. I want him outta my space.

COMMON GROUND STATEMENTS

Especially in Step 3 of the mediation process (Focus on Interests), the basic psychological needs for belonging, power, freedom, and fun often surface as interests the disputants have in common. It is important that disputants understand this common ground in order to come up with **win-win** solutions. It is often necessary for the mediator to make this common ground known because the disputants are focused on their differences and do not hear the common needs expressed. The mediator does this by making **common ground statements**.

For example:

▼ It sounds like you are both angry with a lack of respect shown towards each other, and also both of you don't want to get into any further trouble.

▼ You have both stated that fair treatment and acceptance of your school group is important to you.

▼ I hear you both saying that you have been friends in the past. Do you still want to be friends?

▼ You have each stated that you think the other person is trying to control you. Is it important for you to make your own choices?

CHALLENGING

In some circumstances, it is appropriate for the mediator to question the ideas or attitudes of one or both of the disputants. This might occur if a disputant's statements are put-downs of the other, expressions of prejudice, threats, or unrealistic demands that could escalate the conflict. When the mediator believes the disputant is out of line, he or she will need to **challenge** certain statements respectfully and maintain neutrality.

Wondering

Wondering is a gentle way to challenge:

Disputant: His hair is so messy, and he dresses so sloppy; I can see why he keeps losing things—you should see his locker.

Mediator: I'm wondering how a discussion of clothes and hairstyles will help settle this conflict.

Reality Testing

Reality testing can be used to check the feasibility of ideas or plans:

Disputant: I am going to the Board of Education, and I am going to sue the school.

Mediator: You have every right to be upset and to threaten the board with a lawsuit. However, going to court takes time and may involve spending money. Are there other steps to consider first?

NEGOTIATION

CHOOSING NEGOTIATION

Sometimes you will want to try to resolve conflict without a mediator, either because mediation is not available or because it is not an option you and the other person agree to choose. It is possible to resolve conflicts peacefully by working face-to-face with the other party and without the assistance of a neutral third party. The process is called **negotiation.**

Your understanding of mediation will help you in this process because the six steps are the same. However, negotiation is more difficult than mediation because there is no neutral third party helping disputants work through the steps, communicate with each other, control their anger, or identify common interests. When you serve as a mediator, you are concerned only with the process. When you negotiate, you have a vested interest in the outcome.

You and another student trained as a peer mediator might choose to negotiate a conflict between you. Because you both know how to mediate, you will understand what takes place in each step of the process. But many of your conflicts will be with peers, teachers, or parents who have not received mediation training. When the person you wish to negotiate with does not know the process, these questions and statements will help you begin negotiating:

▼ Can we try to talk about this calmly?

▼ Do you want to work out this problem between us?

▼ Can we cooperate?

▼ Can we make sure we understand the problem before we take action?

▼ I'll listen to you if you will agree to listen to me.

▼ I want to understand your point of view, and I want you to understand my point of view.

These "starter lines" establish the ground rules for the negotiation—take turns talking and listening and cooperate to solve the problem.

Once two individuals agree that they want to negotiate, the steps of the process are the same as they are for mediation. The challenge is for each person to seek to understand the other's point of view and to speak so that his or her point of view can be understood without the help of a neutral third party.

NEGOTIATION PROCESS SUMMARY

STEP 1: AGREE TO NEGOTIATE

▼ I agree to take turns talking and listening and to cooperate to solve the problem.

STEP 2: SHARE POINTS OF VIEW

▼ My view of the problem is _____, and I feel _____.

STEP 3: FOCUS ON INTERESTS

▼ What I want is _____ because _____.

STEP 4: CREATE OPTIONS

▼ Some ideas to solve the problem could be _____.

STEP 5: EVALUATE OPTIONS

▼ Which options will work and be fair for both of us?

STEP 6: CREATE AN AGREEMENT

▼ I am willing to _____.

GROUP PROBLEM SOLVING

CONFLICT AND GROUPS

There are times when conflicts involve groups of people. Organizations, clubs, teams, and cliques can have conflicts internal to the group. Even students in a certain class can have conflicts. Conflicts also occur between different groups. For example:

> The drama club might be preparing for a school play, and there are conflicts between cast members as to practice time and frequency.

> The newspaper staff might be in conflict with the Multicultural Club for publishing an editorial or cartoon that lacked cultural sensitivity.

> Three major school groups have representatives on a planning committee to decide the next school fund-raiser. Each group has its own self-interests and agenda, and these are causing conflict in the planning committee.

> There are conflicts between students in the biology class over scheduling lab times and stations in order to complete the required experiments.

Have groups in this school experienced internal conflict?

What was the conflict?

Was the conflict ever resolved?

Have there been conflicts between groups in the school?

What was the conflict?

Was the conflict resolved?

CHOOSING GROUP PROBLEM SOLVING

Group problem solving is multi-party dispute resolution involving a process of shared decision making. It can be used when the conflict involves more than two people and more than two points of view. The group works to find a consensus decision, or the best solution that the group can make at the time to solve the problem and that can be supported by all members.

The six steps of group problem solving are the same as the six steps of mediation. The group composition in the problem solving can vary from two or three designated spokespersons representing each group or faction of the group to a large group with open participation.

Group problem solving can be very effective, but it is usually more complicated than a two-party mediation, and therefore more time is required. Generally, there will be several points of view and multiple interests. At least two peer mediators, and preferably three or four for large groups, should work together, following the mediation steps, to facilitate problem solving in the group.

GROUND RULES FOR GROUP PROBLEM SOLVING

Managing problem solving in a group is often complex because of the number of participants. Establishing ground rules for the problem-solving session is very important. The following five ground rules are helpful.

1. Participants sit in a circle. This gives no one special status and allows each person to have visual contact with each of the other participants.

2. Every member of the group is responsible for communication—listening and speaking. This means that each person is responsible for sharing his or her point of view if it has not already been shared by another group member and that each person is responsible for working to understand others' points of view.

3. The **rule of focus** applies to all discussions. This means that a speaker will be allowed to talk without being interrupted by other group members.

4. Participants show respect for others. This means no criticism or sarcasm toward group members or their ideas.

5. Each time someone in the group presents a point of view, a group member summarizes that point of view before anyone else can present another point of view.

GROUP PROBLEM SOLVING PROCESS SUMMARY

STEP 1: AGREE TO PROBLEM SOLVE

▼ Group members establish and agree on ground rules.

STEP 2: GATHER POINTS OF VIEW

▼ Group members tell what happened; the problem is identified.

STEP 3: FOCUS ON INTERESTS

▼ Group members tell what they want and why.

STEP 4: CREATE WIN-WIN OPTIONS

▼ Group members brainstorm ideas that will help the whole group.

STEP 5: ESTABLISH CRITERIA AND EVALUATE OPTIONS

▼ Is the solution within the rules?

▼ Is this a decision the group is empowered to make?

▼ Is it fair to all involved?

STEP 6: CREATE AN AGREEMENT

▼ Can each member support this agreement?

▼ What are the specifics of the plan of action?

The questions used in each step of the group problem solving process will generally be the same questions used in the corresponding step of the mediation process.

PROMOTING PEACE

YOUR VIEW OF PEACE

What does Peace mean to you?

What words, images, and feelings do you associate with PEACE?

Where does PEACE occur?

Who is involved when PEACE happens?

PEACE WHEEL

Record your own ideas about peace on the Peace Wheel.

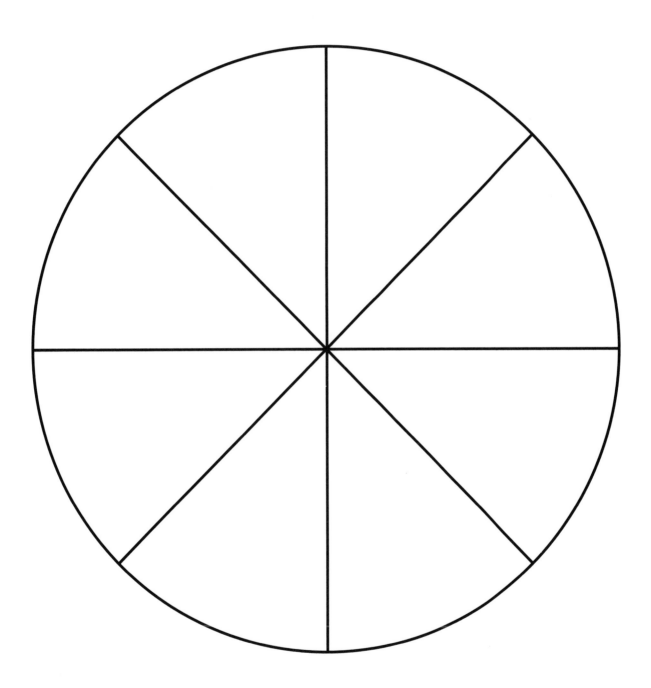

Peer Mediation Forms

PEER MEDIATION REQUEST

Date_____

Names of students in conflict:

_____ Grade _____

_____ Grade _____

_____ Grade _____

_____ Grade _____

Where did the conflict occur? *(check one)*

❑ Bus   ❑ Outdoors

❑ Cafeteria   ❑ Gym/locker room

❑ Classroom   ❑ Bathroom

❑ Hallway

❑ Other *(specify)* _____

Briefly describe the problem:

_____

_____

_____

_____

Mediation requested by *(check one)*

❑ Student   ❑ Social worker

❑ Teacher   ❑ Dean/assistant principal

❑ Counselor   ❑ Principal

❑ Other *(specify)* _____

Signature of person requesting mediation _____

DO NOT WRITE BELOW THIS LINE
TO BE COMPLETED BY A PROGRAM COORDINATOR

What is the conflict about? *(check one)*

❑ Rumors   ❑ Fighting or hitting

❑ Harassment   ❑ Bias or prejudice

❑ Threats   ❑ Relationship

❑ Name-calling   ❑ Property loss or damage

❑ Other *(specify)* _____

BRAINSTORMING WORKSHEET

OPTIONS LIST

▼ What are some possible options that address both of your interests?

▼ What other possibilities can you think of?

1. _____

2. _____

3. _____

4. _____

5. _____

6. _____

7. _____

8. _____

9. _____

10. _____

PEER MEDIATION AGREEMENT

Date_____

We voluntarily participated in a mediation. We have reached an agreement that we believe is fair and that solves the problem between us. In the future if we have problems that we cannot resolve on our own, we agree to come back to mediation.

Name _____   Name _____

_____   _____

_____   _____

_____   _____

_____   _____

_____   _____

_____   _____

_____   _____

_____   _____

_____   _____

_____   _____

_____   _____

Signature _____   Signature _____

Mediator signature _____

Mediator signature _____

PEER MEDIATOR CONTRACT

As a peer mediator, I understand my role is to help students resolve conflict peacefully. As a peer mediator, I agree to the following terms.

1. To complete basic and advanced training sessions at the scheduled times

2. To maintain privacy for all mediations

3. To be a responsible peer mediator by conducting mediation sessions according to the process, completing all necessary forms, and promoting the program

4. To maintain satisfactory school conduct (this includes using mediation services for interpersonal conflicts)

5. To make up any class work missed during training or mediation sessions

6. To serve as a peer mediator for the year

Student signature _____ Date _____

Date _____

Mediator _____

Mediator _____

Place a check mark (✓) by each step where you did quality work. Place an asterisk (*) by each step where you think the quality could improve. Co-mediators complete this form as a team.

STEP 1: AGREE TO MEDIATE

❏ Welcomed both people and introduced yourself as the mediator.

❏ Explained the mediation process.

❏ Explained ground rules.

❏ Asked each person: "Are you willing to follow the rules?"

STEP 2: GATHER POINTS OF VIEW

❏ Asked each person to tell what happened.

❏ Listened, summarized, clarified.

STEP 3: FOCUS ON INTERESTS

❏ Found real interests.

❏ Listened, summarized, clarified.

❏ Summarized interests before going to the next step.

STEP 4: CREATE WIN-WIN OPTIONS

❏ Explained brainstorming rules.

❏ Asked for ideas that address the interests of both parties.

STEP 5: EVALUATE OPTIONS

❏ Asked parties to combine options or parts of options.

❏ For each option, asked:

Is this option fair?

Can you do it?

Do you think it will work?

STEP 6: CREATE AN AGREEMENT

❏ Asked disputants to make a plan of action: Who, what, when, where, how?

❏ Wrote the plan.

❏ Asked each person to read the plan and sign the agreement.

❏ Closed the session with a handshake.

OTHER

❏ Remained neutral—did not take sides.

❏ Avoided making suggestions to solve the problem.

❏ If parties did not reach an agreement, knew what to say to end the session.

❏ Worked together with co-mediator.

❏ Gave each party a turn to talk without interruption.

Answer the following questions.

1. What did you do well?

2. If you could do this mediation again, what might you do differently?

3. Were certain steps more difficult for you than others? If so, what could you do to strengthen these steps?

4. Do you have any other concerns or questions?

Staff supervisor _____ Date _____

Comments:

Glossary

ACTIVE LISTENING: Actively seeking to understand the message of another by using the skills of attending, summarizing, and clarifying

AGGRESSION: Forceful action or attack

APOLOGIZING: To admit error or discourtesy by an expression of regret

ASSERTION: Expressing one's needs and wants in a way that shows respect for others' needs and wants

ATTENDING: Using mostly nonverbal behaviors such as eye contact, gestures, and facial expressions to indicate interest in the speaker's message

AVOID: To keep away from, stay clear of, shun

BASIC NEEDS: Needs that underlie all human behavior (belonging, power, freedom, fun)

BATNA: The Best Alternative to a Negotiated Agreement, or a personal assessment useful in deciding whether to negotiate (mediate) and a standard for determining if an agreement is acceptable

BEHAVE: To act, function, or conduct oneself in a specific way

BELONGING: A feeling of being part of a group or in natural association with others (one of the four basic needs)

BIAS: A predetermined and often prejudiced view

BRAINSTORMING: A technique for helping disputants create as many options as they can for solving their problems

CAUCUS: Meeting with each disputant individually

CHOICE: Option of selection; power of deciding

CLARIFY: To make clearer or easier to understand

CLIQUE: A group of individuals drawn together by some common interest and exclusive of others

COMBINE: To bring into a state of unity, join, merge, or blend; to join forces for a common purpose or enter into an alliance

COMMUNICATE: To express thoughts, feelings, and actions so they are understood

COMMUNITY: A social group having common interests; similarity or identity among people

COMPROMISE: A settlement of differences in which each side makes concessions

CONFIDENTIAL: Secret; communicated to another under the assurance it will not be repeated

CONFLICT: Controversy or disagreement; to come into opposition

CONFRONT: To face with hostility or oppose defiantly

CONSEQUENCE: That which logically or naturally follows an action

CONTROL: To direct, guide, or influence

COOPERATION: Associating for mutual benefit; working toward a common end or purpose

CREATE: To bring into being, originate, or produce

CRITERION: Standard; a basis for judging

CULTURAL DIVERSITY: Differences in individuals attributed to race, religion, or ethnicity

DEESCALATE: To decrease the intensity of

DIFFERENCE: The condition or degree of being unlike, dissimilar, or diverse

DISAGREEMENT: A failure or refusal to agree; a difference of opinion

DISCRIMINATION: An act based on prejudice

DISPUTANT: One engaged in an argument or conflict

DIVERSITY: The fact or quality of being different or distinct

EMOTION: A strong feeling (for example, joy, sorrow, reverence, hate, love)

EMPATHIC: Characterized by understanding so intimate that the feelings, thoughts, and actions of one are easily known by another

ESCALATE: To increase or intensify

ETHNIC: Relating to large groups of people classed according to common racial, national, or cultural background

FREEDOM: The capacity to exercise choice or free will (one of the four basic needs)

FUN: Enjoyment, pleasure, amusement, playful behavior (one of the four basic needs)

GROUND RULE: One of several basic rules for conducting peer mediation, spelled out to disputants at the beginning of the session

HIDDEN INTEREST: In a conflict situation, a basic need or want people may have that does not appear on the surface to be related to the problem

HOSTILITY: State of being antagonistic; hatred

INTEREST: Involvement or concern; the aspect of something that enables it to matter

INTOLERANCE: Quality or condition of being unable to grant equal freedom of expression; bigotry

MEDIATE: To intervene between two or more disputing parties in order to bring about an agreement

MISUNDERSTANDING: A failure to understand; a disagreement

NEGOTIATE: To discuss with another or others in order to come to terms or reach an agreement

OPTION: Something that may be chosen; an alternative course of action

PASSIVE AGGRESSION: An indirect expression of one's anger (for example, by refusing to cooperate)

PEACE: A process of responding to diversity and conflict with tolerance, imagination, and flexibility; fully exercising one's responsibilities to ensure that all fully enjoy all human rights

PEACEMAKING: Honoring self, honoring others, and honoring the environment

PEER MEDIATION: A process of conflict resolution, facilitated by a neutral, trained peer mediator, in which students work together to solve their own problems

PERCEPTION: The process or act of insight, intuition, or knowledge gained through the senses

POSITION: A mental posture or point of view

POWER: The ability to act or perform effectively (one of the four basic needs)

PREJUDICE: An adverse judgment or opinion formed without knowledge or examination of facts; irrational suspicion or hatred for a particular group, race, or religion; the holding of preconceived judgments

PRIVATE: Not available for public knowledge

RECONCILE: To reestablish friendship between; to settle or resolve

RESOLUTION: A course of action decided upon to solve a problem

RESOURCE: An available supply that can be drawn upon when needed

RESPECT: To feel or show esteem for; to honor

RESPONSIBILITY: Personal accountability or the ability to act without guidance

SOCIAL DIVERSITY: Differences in individuals attributed to gender, sexual orientation, social class, or physical/mental abilities

STEREOTYPE: A mental picture that reflects an oversimplified judgment about something or someone

SUMMARIZE: To restate in a brief, concise form

SYNERGY: Action of two or more people working together to achieve something neither could achieve alone

TRUST: To have confidence in or feel sure of; faith

UNDERSTAND: To perceive and comprehend the nature and significance of; to know and be tolerant or sympathetic toward

VALUE: A principle, standard, or quality considered worthwhile or desirable; to regard highly

VIOLENCE: Actual or threatened use of physical force toward another